Social Studies for Prim Grade 1 Workbook

Myself, My Family, My School

Compiled by
Cynthia Smith and Geneva Gibson

All Rights Reserved. No part of this publication may be reproduced, stored in a retrieval system, or transmitted, in any form or by any means, electronic, mechanical, photocopying, recording, or otherwise, without the prior permission in writing of the author and publisher.

The author and publisher are still awaiting a response from some copyright owners and will acknowledge permission at the first opportunity.

Table of Contents

Using this book…………………………………………………………………………3

Theme 1: Myself
All about me……………………………………………………………………………4
Am I like…?……………………………………………………………………………6
My country……………………………………………………………………………8
My needs………………………………………………………………………………10
What do I like to do?…………………………………………………………………12
I am part of a group…………………………………………………………………14
Let us share the work………………………………………………………………16
Respect others………………………………………………………………………18
Being helpful to visitors……………………………………………………………20

Theme 2: My Family
Families………………………………………………………………………………22
Needing each other…………………………………………………………………24
A job for everyone……………………………………………………………………26
Leisure …………………………………………………………………………………28
My House……………………………………………………………………………30
Rules of the home……………………………………………………………………32
Safety in the home……………………………………………………………………34
Caring for our home…………………………………………………………………36
Theme 2: What have you learned?…………………………………………………38

Theme 3: My School
Going to school………………………………………………………………………40
Take care on the street………………………………………………………………42
What is our school like?……………………………………………………………44
People who work in our school……………………………………………………46
School rules…………………………………………………………………………48
The name of our school……………………………………………………………50
Activities at school……………………………………………………………………52
Taking care of our school……………………………………………………………54
Entertaining our visitors……………………………………………………………56
Theme 3: What have you learned?…………………………………………………60

Work Cited……………………………………………………………………………61

Using this Book

This workbook is to be used in conjunction with The Bahamas' Ministry of Education first grade curriculum. All of the topics and relevant notes came from the curriculum. Teachers should teach the lessons first to students and then allow them to answer the questions about each topic.

The following should be taken into consideration when teaching the lessons in this book.

- Students are engaged in hands-on activities so that they can see the practical part of the lessons.
- Field trips should be taken where possible.
- Guest speakers should be invited to share their knowledge of the topic/s.
- Lots of visuals should be used when teaching the lessons.

To be better able to deliver an engaging lesson, teachers can go to the website:

bahamaseducationtionalexpress@teacherpayteacher.com

bahamaseducationtionalexpress@thestudentshed.org

https://www.youtube.com/feed/my_videos

On these sites, you will find the following:
- video lessons for all lessons in this book
- foldable for all lessons
- GLAT past papers
- Additional worksheets for lessons

Remember teachers, *"children learn by doing."* It is our prayer that you enjoy using this book to help educate the students of our Bahama Land.

All About Me

I am special. God made me in His own image. I live with my family.

I attend primary school. I am five (5/6) years old.

Directions: Complete the sentences.

My name is _____.

I am a _____.

I am _____ years old.

My birthday is _____.

My telephone number is _____.

Am I Like?

Our hair, skin, eyes, size, and height are different. Some people have black, brown, or blond hair. The skin can be dark or light brown. People can be short, tall, thin, small, or big. Children are born every day all over the world.

Directions:

1.   Colour the hair black
Colour the skin brown
Write one sentence about the picture.

_____

_____

My Country

The Bahamas is made up of many islands. I live on the island of

_____. Bahamians are friendly people. I am

proud to be a Bahamian.

Directions: Choose the correct answer.

1. Circle the colours in the Bahamian flag.

aquamarine   red   gold   black

2. I am _____ to be a Bahamian.

3. The Bahamas is made up of _____ islands. (1)

4. I live on the island of _____.

5. Colour the flag.

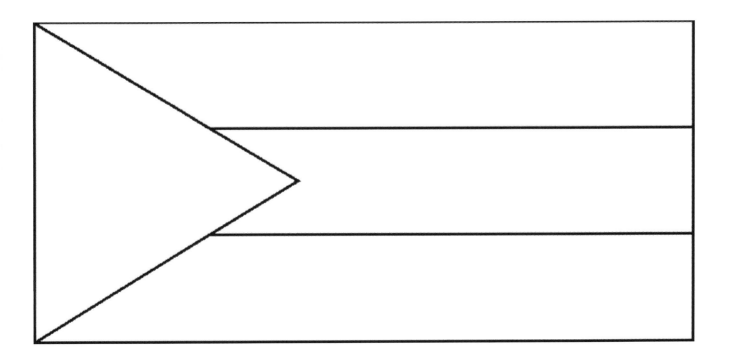

My Needs

Our basic needs are food, love, shelter, and clothes.

1. Circle pictures that show our needs.

2. Draw a box around the pictures of the food we eat.

3. Circle the pictures of places to live in.

 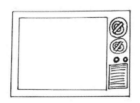 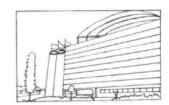

4. Circle the pictures that show love.

5. Colour the pictures of clothes.

What I Like to Do

There are many different hobbies. Some people like dancing, reading, playing basketball, swimming, and flying kites.

1. Circle pictures that show what you know how to do.

Write a sentence to tell what you like to do.

_____

_____

I Am Part of a Group

People belong to many different groups. Some groups are church choirs, bands, school families, Girls Guide, and Boys Brigade.

Directions: Match the name with the correct picture.

band

choir

classroom

Let us Share the Work

Everyone should share the work at home. Working together makes the job easier.

Directions: Circle pictures that show how you share the work at home.

Respect Others

Do unto others as you will have them do unto you. When you respect others, others will respect you. Be kind to everyone.

Directions:

1. Colour the picture that shows students being kind.

2. Mark an X on the picture where students are not kind.

Being Helpful to Others

Visitors are people who visit from other countries. Tourists are another name for visitors. Visitors sometimes revisit some countries. People should be kind to visitors.

Directions: Write 'T' for True or 'F' for False to complete each sentence.

1. Visitors are people who visit from other countries. _____

2. Visitor is another name for tourists. _____

3. Sometimes tourists come back to our country. _____

4. We should fight our tourists. _____

5. Visitors are not nice people. _____

Families

There are many different kinds of family structures (nuclear, extended families)

Nuclear family is a family that includes only the father, mother, and children

An extended family is simply a family unit that extends past the nuclear family to include other relatives such as aunts, uncles, and grandparents.

1. Write a sentence to tell what your family is like.

_____

_____

2. Draw the face of each family member that lives in your house on an apple.

23

Needing each other

Members of a family need each other.

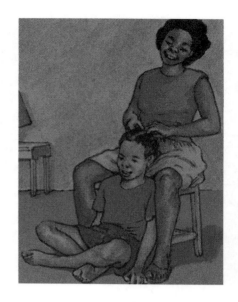

1. Tell how you need your family.

_____

_____

_____

2. Tell how your family needs you.

_____

_____

_____

A Job for Everyone

Every member of the family must work.
They help to get things the family needs.

Father is a plumber

Mother works at the hotel

Sister is a chemist

Jean and Tom have special jobs too. They help with the work at home

1. What are the jobs that the members of your family do? List them.
_____
_____
_____
_____

2. Write the names of these jobs that members of the family do.

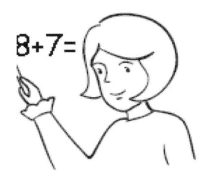

_____

_____

_____

_____

Leisure

Families can have fun together.

1. Make a drawing showing you and your family having fun.

My House

There are many types of houses. Look at these houses. Talk about them.

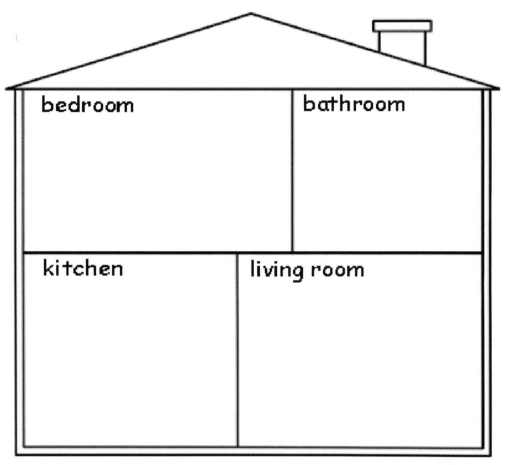

1. Name the rooms in your house.

_____

_____

_____

_____

2. What are these rooms used for?

_____

_____

_____

3. Which room do you like the best?

_____

Rules of the Home

Every family has rules they follow. Our country and school have rules. Rules help to keep us safe.

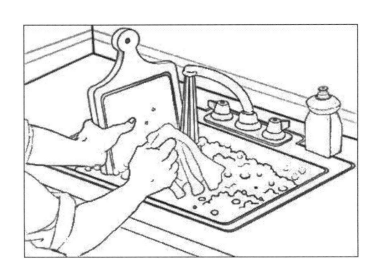

1. Write TWO sentences about the rules in your family.

_____

_____

_____

_____

Safety in the Home

Danger comes in different forms. In order to avoid danger, rules need to be put in place to keep everyone safe.

1. Colour the pictures that show danger at home.

2. Circle the picture that shows safety at home.

Caring for Your Home

We must keep our environment clean. This will help keep germs away, and we will be healthy.

1. Colour the picture to show how you care for your home.

2. Write two rules you can do to care for your home.
_____
_____
_____
_____

What Have You Learned?

Complete these sentences.

1. _____ is a danger

2. Members _____ of my _____ need each other.

3. _____ your hands before meals.

4. There are many types of _____

5. We sleep in the _____

38

Going to School

School is a child's family away from the family. It fills some needs of a child that a family cannot fulfill. Here the child learns formal and informal education.

At school, a child develops educationally, socially, physically, and spiritually. The main lesson helps a child how to get along in the world.

The names of famous persons or communities identify schools. The school system is made up of rules and regulations.

1. List three public buildings you see on your way to school.

_____

_____

2. Circle the action to show how you get to school.

3. Who is your school name after?

_____

_____

Take Care on the Street

Here are some rules to follow when walking on the streets.

1. Walk to the side of the street away from traffic.

2. Walk-in single file.

3. Cross the street where there is a pedestrian crossing on or crossing guard.

4. Wear light colour clothing at night.

5. Wait until the traffic stops before crossing the street.

6. To cross the street carefully. Look left, look right. Look left again.

1. Draw a picture to show how you cross the street.

What is Your School Like?

A school can be small or large, one building or more than one building, one story or two stories. Schools can be primary, junior, and secondary.

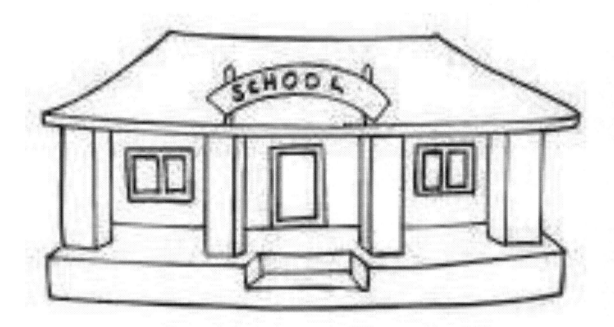

1. What school do you attend?

_____

_____

2. Draw and colour your school building.

3. On your picture, label your classroom, school's office, and music room.

People Who Work in Our School

Many people work at my school. They have different jobs such as principal, secretary, librarian, teacher, janitress, security guard, and a yardman.

1. What is the job of any three people at your school? (Write a sentence for each.)

_____

_____

_____

2. Write the words teacher, janitor, principal, and lunch vendor next to each picture.

_____   _____

_____   _____

School Rules

School rules are made as a guide and reminder for students.

> School Rules
>
> Be polite
>
> Be neat and tidy.
>
> Always walk quietly.
>
> Put trash in bins.
>
> Do not throw objects.
>
> No fighting.

1. Write TWO new rules for the school.

_____

_____

_____

_____

The Name of Your School

A school can be named after a person or a settlement. This is the statue of Woodes Rogers in New Providence. A school is named after him.

1. Find out who your school is named after. Write it on the line.

_____

_____

2. Write two sentences about who your school is named after.

_____

_____

_____

_____

Activities at School

At school, we do lots of different things e.g., exercise, play, write, sing, draw or colour.

1. Look at each picture. Write a sentence to tell what is happening in each picture.

_____

_____

_____

_____

Taking Care of Your School

Each child must help to take care of their school. Children can clean tables, and chalkboards, mop the floor, pick up papers, and plant and water flowers.

1. Look at the picture below. Write two sentences about the picture.

_____
_____
_____
_____

2. Write the names of two flowers you can find in a garden.

_____   _____

Entertaining Our Visitors

We should always be kind and friendly to visitors. When visitors visit our school, we should know how to greet them. Visitors can be your parents, friends, and officials from the government.

1. Make a list of FOUR activities that you can do to entertain guests.

_____

_____

_____

_____

What Have You Learned?

1. Describe your school to a friend.

> Use these words:
> teacher, traffic, classroom, jobs, care, rule, things, school, visitors, principal, street, home

Work Cited

Department of Education. (1997). *Commonwealth of The Bahamas, Ministry of Education Social Studies Curriculum Guideline*s (Grade Levels 1 and 2)

Made in the USA
Middletown, DE
26 July 2024

58033613R00035